CapitaLogic Limited

Empowering Wealth and Capital

I0484199

A Practitioner's Guide To Target Accrual Redemption Forwards (Second Edition)

Jointly authored by:

Dr. Yat-fai LAM, Doctor of Business Administration (Finance), CFA, CAIA, FRM, PRM

Prof. Kin-keung LAI, PhD in Transportation Engineering and Operations Research

Printed in the United States of America.

Yat-fai LAM
Kin-keung LAI

   A Practitioner's Guide To Target Accrual Redemption Forwards (2nd ed.)

   ISBN-13: 978-1507645246
   ISBN-10: 1507645244

   1. Derivatives   2. Structured Products
   3. Target Accrual Redemption Forwards

Preface

Target accrual redemption forwards are the most popular currency structured products among corporate and private banking customers. This investment product facilitates an investor to hedge his currency exposure at a lower cost or speculate on the direction of a currency rate with lower upfront cash outflow.

Nevertheless, the technical details behind target accrual redemption forwards have never been elaborated with sufficient granularity in any public documents. This results in a material mis-communications among treasury marketing, corporate sales, risk management and investors.

This book takes the first step in the financial industry to explain the technical details of target accrual redemption forwards in simple terms so as to unify the understanding among various stakeholders.

About the Authors

Dr. Yat-fai LAM (林日輝 博士)

Dr. Yat-fai LAM is the Adjunct Assistant Professor of Finance at The University of Hong Kong, the MSc Dissertation Supervisor of the postgraduate programmes conducted in Hong Kong by The University of Warwick and the Adjunct Faculty of Finance at City University of Hong Kong. Dr. LAM has worked for bank regulator, international bank, asset management firm, financial advisory firm and credit rating agency, specializing in structured products, credit risk management and Basel III framework.

Dr. LAM graduated from City University of Hong Kong with a Doctor of Business Administration (Finance) degree. He holds the CFA, CAIA, FRM and PRM designations issued by the CFA Institute, CAIA Association, GARP and PRMIA respectively. Also, Dr. LAM is honoured with the "PRM Award of Merit 2005" by PRMIA for his outstanding results in the PRM examination.

Prof. Kin-keung LAI (黎建強 讲座教授)

Prof. Kin-keung LAI received his PhD at Michigan State University, USA. He is currently the Chair Professor of Management Science at City University of Hong Kong. Prior to his academic career, Prof. LAI was a Senior Operational Research Analyst of Cathay Pacific Airways and an Area Manager on Marketing Information Systems of Union Carbide Eastern. Professor LAI's main areas of researches are operations and supply chain management, financial and business risk analysis, and modeling using computational intelligence.

Prof. LAI was the recipient of the Joon S. Moon Distinguished International Alumni Award of the Michigan State University and also appointed as the Chang Jiang Scholar Chair Professor by the Ministry of Education, China. He was ranked as the top four academic author in the area of business intelligence and analytics worldwide by MIS Quarterly Special Issue in 2012. Most recently, Prof. LAI receives the Civil and Environmental Engineering Distinguished Alumni Award, Michigan State University, USA.

Contents

1   Introduction 6

2   Functional purposes 6

3   Structuring... 6

4   Zero value TARF 9

5   Specification.. 11

6   Cash flows.. 12

7   Revenue model.. 14

8   Sales and marketing 15

9   Valuation.. 17

10   Risk analysis 20

11   Derivative accounting 24

12   Variations of TARF... 24

Appendix 1   Sample fixing ticket 32

Appendix 2   Sample deal confirmation.......................... 33

References.. 37

1   Introduction

A target accrual redemption forward ("TARF") is a currency structured product developed for an investor to hedge his currency exposure at a lower cost or speculate in the direction of a currency rate with lower upfront cash outflow. It is a very popular investment product among corporate and private banking customers. A TARF belongs to the participation category of structured products under the classification scheme of Swiss Structured Products Association.

This book describes in simple terms the major technical aspects of TARFs in order to facilitate the understanding of this structured product.

2   Functional purposes

A TARF is initially designed to hedge a currency exposure at a lower cost. The strike rate, notional principals and bonus target are customized to meet an investor's expectation on the movement of a currency rate during the investment period.

A TARF also allows an investor to speculate in the direction of a currency rate with a lower upfront cash outflow. The early termination feature offers the investor to roll over to a new TARF in accordance with the latest market conditions when an existing TARF has reached its profit target.

A TARF is relatively easy to be synthesized with liquidly traded currency options. This makes the hedging of a TARF efficient and effective. The early termination feature minimizes the hedging cost of a TARF issuer when the currency rate has demonstrated consistently along a direction unfavourable to the issuer.

3   Structuring

A TARF is synthesized with three major components:

- a series of call options with payoff function

  $$\text{Max[Current rate - Strike rate, 0]} \times \text{Call notional principal}$$

- a series of put options with payoff function

  $$\text{Max[Strike rate - Current rate, 0]} \times \text{Put notional principal}$$

- an early termination feature.

3.1   Bull structure

If an investor expects that

- a currency tends to appreciate during an investment period; and

- the currency rate is unlikely to drop below a boundary K during the investment period,

he may enter a bull TARF which comprises

- a series of long positions in call options at various maturities of regular time intervals, with the same notional principal and strike rate K; and

- a series of short positions in put options with (i) the same maturities and strike rate as the call options; and (ii) a notional principal larger than that of the call options.

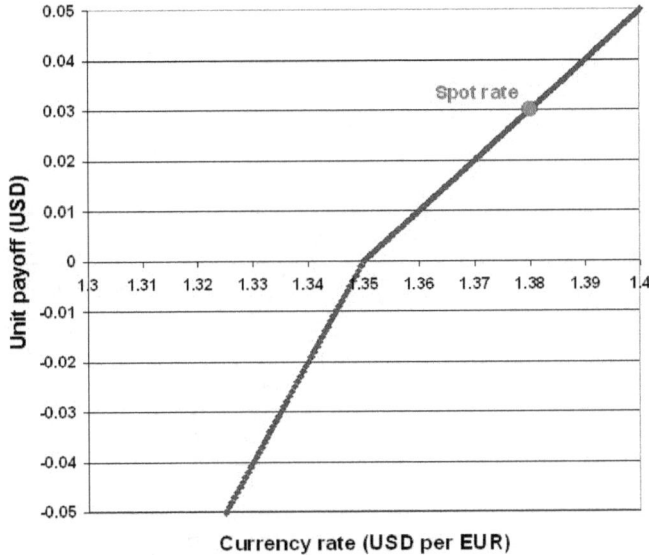

Figure 3.1   Unit payoff of a bull TARF

In addition, a bonus target is set out such that in case the aggregated payoff from the call options reaches the bonus target, the entire TARF terminates automatically.

3.2   Bear structure

If an investor expects that

- a currency tends to depreciate during an investment period; and

- the currency rate is unlikely to rise above a boundary K during the investment period,

he may enter a bear TARF which comprises

- a series of long positions in put options at various maturities of regular time intervals, with the same notional principal and strike rate K; and

- a series of short positions in call options with (i) the same maturities and strike rate as the put options; and (ii) a notional principal larger than that of the put options.

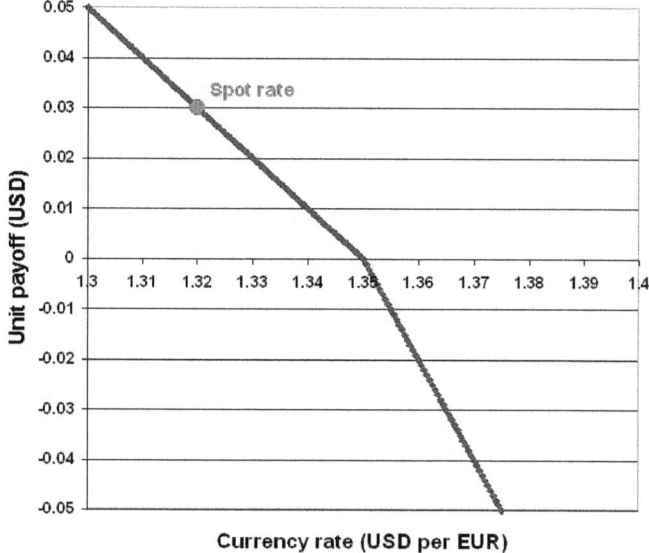

Figure 3.2 Unit payoff of a bear TARF

In addition, a bonus target is set out such that in case the aggregated payoff from the put options reaches the bonus target, the entire TARF terminates automatically.

4   Zero value TARF

A TARF with zero value at origination is particularly welcome to many investors and issuers since neither party needs to pay any upfront cash outflows.

Central to the construction of a zero value TARF is the idea of offsetting the cost of acquiring in-the-money ("ITM") options with the revenue from writing out-of-the-money ("OTM") options.

4.1   In-the-money option

A call option is ITM if the spot currency rate is above the strike rate. A put option is ITM if the spot currency rate is below the strike rate. With an ITM option, the position of the spot currency rate is inline with the expectation of an investor. An ITM option has a higher chance to result in a positive payoff at maturity, therefore subject to a moderate value. The value of an ITM option increases with increasing difference between the spot currency rate and strike rate.

4.2   Out-of-the-money option

A call option is OTM if the spot currency rate is below the strike rate. A put option is OTM if the spot currency rate is above the strike rate. With an OTM option, the position of the spot currency rate is against the expectation of an investor. An OTM option has a higher chance to result in a zero payoff at maturity, therefore subject to a lower value. The value of an OTM option decreases with increasing difference between the strike currency rate and spot rate.

4.3   Zero value bull TARF

If an investor expects that a currency will appreciate during an investment period, he acquires a series of call options. In order to enhance the potential that the call options will result in positive payoff at maturity, the strike rate is set substantially lower than the spot currency rate. These call options are then ITM and must be acquired at a higher cost. In order to offset the cost of these call options, the investor writes a series of put options with the same strike rate and maturities as the call options. These put options are then OTM and subject to a lower value. In order to match the two sets of option values, the put notional principal must be significantly larger than the call notional principal. Nevertheless, a large put notional principal means that the investor is subject to the risk of paying a large amount to the acquirers of the put options in case the put options mature at a currency rate well below the strike rate. To control this downside risk, the total profit from the series of call options is limited by a bonus target. As the upside profit is limited, the put notional principal could be reduced, subject to the condition that the bull TARF is constructed at a zero value. Under such arrangement, if the strike rate is fixed, the put notional principal increases with increasing bonus target.

During the structuring of many bull TARFs, the strike rate is set according to the investor's view on the lower boundary of the movement of the currency rate during the investment period, the put notional principal is equal to twice the call notional principal and the bonus target is selected to result in a near zero TARF value.

4.4   Zero value bear TARF

If an investor expects that a currency will depreciate during an investment period, he acquires a series of put options. In order to enhance the potential that the put options will result in positive payoff at maturity, the strike rate is set substantially higher than the spot currency rate. These put options are then ITM and must be acquired at a higher cost. In order to offset the cost of these put options, the investor writes a series of call options with the same strike rate and maturities as the put options. These call options are then OTM and subject to a lower value. In order to match the two sets of option values, the call notional principal must be significantly larger than the put notional principal. Nevertheless, a large call notional principal means that the investor is subject to the risk of paying a large amount to the acquirers of the call options in case the call options mature at a currency rate well above the strike rate. To control this downside risk, the total profit from the series of put options is limited by a bonus target. As the upside profit is limited, the call notional principal could be reduced, subject to the condition that the bear TARF is constructed at a zero value. Under such arrangement, if the strike rate is fixed, the call notional principal increases with increasing bonus target.

During the structuring of many bear TARFs, the strike rate is set according to the investor's view on the upper boundary of the movement of the currency rate during the investment period, the call notional principal is equal to twice the put notional principal and the bonus target is selected to result in a near zero TARF value.

5   Specification

A TARF is specified by the following major parameters:

(a) Domestic currency

The domestic currency is the base currency in which the option transactions are denominated. The profits and losses are calculated in domestic currency.

(b) Foreign currency

The foreign currency is the underlying currency to which the performances of the component options are linked.

(c) Call notional principal

The call notional principal is the notional principal of the component call options. All component call options share the same notional principal.

(d) Put notional principal

The put notional principal is the notional principal of the component put options. All component put options share the same notional principal.

(e) Settlement approach

The payoffs of the call and put options can be settled in either domestic currency or foreign currency. Please refer to section 6.2 for detailed explanations.

(f) Strike rate

The strike rate is the currency rate

- over which a component call option will generate positive payoff on its maturity day; or

- under which a component put option will generate positive payoff on its maturity day.

All component options share the same strike rate.

(g) Fixing frequency

A pair of call and put options with the same strike rate and maturity day is referred to as a fixing. Hence the maturity day of a fixing is also referred to as a fixing day. The fixing frequency specifies the regular time interval between the fixing days of any two consecutive fixings. Most TARFs are constructed with fixings on monthly basis.

(h) Maturity day

The maturity day of a TARF is equal to the fixing day of the last pair of component options.

(i) Bonus target

The payoff from the long position of a component option in a TARF is referred to as a bonus. The bonus target is the amount of aggregated bonus over which a TARF will terminate automatically.

(j) Treatment to termination bonus

If the bonus target is met after a particular bonus is aggregated, this bonus is referred to as a termination bonus. There are two alternative treatments to the termination bonus:

- the investor will receive the full amount of the termination bonus; or

- the investor will receive part of the termination bonus such that the aggregated bonus received will be equal to the bonus target.

6   Cash flows

The cash flows of a TARF include the initial cash flow when a TARF is originated and the subsequent interim cash flows on the second trading day after a fixing day.

6.1   Initial cash flow

An investor pays an initial cash outflow, referred to as TARF price, to acquire a TARF. This initial cash outflow comprises the value of the TARF, the operating cost and the profit to issuer.

An investor pays only the operating cost and the profit to issuer in order to acquire a zero value TARF. Taking one step further, if the value of the TARF is sufficiently negative due to the large notional principal of the short OTM option positions, the investor may receive at origination an initial cash inflow which is attractive to many investors.

6.2 Interim cash flows

Interim cash flows are received and/or paid by the investor two trading days after a fixing day. If the investor specifies that the interim cash flows are settled in domestic currency, the cash flows are delivered according to the scheme set out in Table 6.1.

Currency rate	Bull TARF	Bear TARF
> strike rate	Investor receives from issuer a cash inflow in domestic currency equal to the payoff of the call option.	Investor delivers to issuer a cash outflow in domestic currency equal to the payoff of the call option.
< strike rate	Investor delivers to issuer a cash outflow in domestic currency equal to the payoff of the put option.	Investor receives from issuer a cash inflow in domestic currency equal to the payoff of the put option.

Table 6.1   Interim cash flows of a TARF settled in domestic currency

If the investor specifies that the interim cash flows are settled in foreign currency, the cash flows are delivered according to the scheme set out in Table 6.2

Currency rate	Bull TARF	Bear TARF
> strike rate	Investor acquires from issuer the foreign currency with an amount equal to the call notional principal at a strike rate lower than the spot currency rate on the fixing day.	Investor sells to issuer the foreign currency with an amount equal to the call notional principal at a strike rate lower than the spot currency rate on the fixing day.
< strike rate	Investor acquires from issuer the foreign currency with an amount equal to the put notional principal at a strike rate higher than the spot currency rate on the fixing day.	Investor sells to issuer the foreign currency with an amount equal to the put notional principal at a strike rate higher than the spot currency rate on the fixing day.

Table 6.2   Interim cash flows of a TARF settled in foreign currency

The positive payoff received by the investor is referred to as bonus. These bonuses are aggregated over the life of the TARF. If the aggregated amount of the bonus is equal to or above the bonus target after a particular bonus, the TARF is terminated automatically after that fixing day.

The termination bonus will be received in full or in part, subject to the termination condition of the TARF.

6.3   Scenario analysis

Table 6.3 shows the major parameters of an example bull TARF.

	Parameter	Value
1.	Domestic currency	USD
2.	Foreign currency	EUR
3.	Call notional principal	EUR 1,000,000
4.	Put notional principal	EUR 2,000,000
5.	Settlement approach	Foreign currency
6.	Strike rate	USD 1.3500 per EUR
7.	Maturity date	19 December 2014
8.	Fixing frequency	Monthly
9.	Bonus target	USD 136,000
10.	Treatment to termination bonus	Full payment

Table 6.3   An example bull TARF

On a fixing day, if the currency rate is USD 1.3603 per EUR, then the investor buy from the issuer EUR 1,000,000 at a favourable rate USD 1.3500 per EUR. In other words, the investor is subject to a profit

$$1,000,000 \times (1.3603 - 1.3500) = USD\ 10,300$$

Conversely, on a fixing day, if the currency rate is USD 1.3471 per EUR, then the investor must buy from the issuer EUR 2,000,000 at an unfavourable rate USD 1.3500 per EUR. In other words, the investor is subject to a loss

$$2,000,000 \times (1.3500 - 1.3471) = USD\ 5,800$$

7   Revenue model

An investment bank with a strong technical expertise may synthesize a TARF with underlying currency and liquidly traded options at a lower cost and sells to a commercial bank at a higher price after incorporating the operating cost and profit.

A commercial bank with a strong customer base may acquire a TARF from an investment bank at a lower cost and sells to an investor at a higher price after incorporating the additional layer of operating cost and profit.

In contrast to many other financial instruments, the TARF is operated in a one way market. In other words, an investor cannot sell a TARF to an investment bank or a commercial bank.

8   Sales and marketing

Commercial banks approach corporate and private banking customers pro-actively to promote the investments in the TARFs. A TARF investor, in general, has had a longer term relationship with a commercial bank which accepts the assets and financial instruments deposited to the bank as collaterals to establish an margin amount. The investor then utilizes the margin amount to support the investments in the TARFs without any physical funding from investors.

There are four major factors that drive the marketing of TARFs:

- The attractive product features of a TARF;
- The professional sales team which performs the marketing;
- The price of a TARF; and
- The post sales customer services.

8.1   Product features

In general, an investor prefers a structured product

- that matches his risk-return preference;
- that conform to his foreign currency exposures;
- with no or only small initial cash outflow; and
- preferably with some initial cash inflow.

A TARF, by construction, can easily be tailed to match these requirements.

Nevertheless, attractive features always come with a cost. The higher potential profit is subject to a higher risk and the initial cash inflow is backed up by the potential subsequent cash outflows on payment dates.

8.2   Professional sales team

Since a TARF is a relatively sophisticated investment product with complex cash flows, a strong sales team with professional knowledge to promote the TARF to investors is critical to the success of the TARF marketing.

The professional sales team needs to identify the needs and preferences of an investor, propose appropriate TARF structure and explain to an investor in simple terms the advantages and concerns of a TARF. In some situations where a currency rate moves against the expectation of an investor who has invested in a TARF, the professional sales team needs to propose strategies to limit the loss of the investor.

Due to the complexity of a TARF, it is rare that an investor could understand clearly every single technical detail of a TARF. The professional sales team then plays the role of a safeguard to provide advice to the investor. Therefore, the confidence to the professional sales team from an investor is the single most important factor to maintain the customer relationship.

8.3   Price of a TARF

The price of a TARF comprises the value of the TARF, the operating cost and the profit to issuer. A lower TARF price is always welcome to an investor. Nevertheless, due to competition among issuers, the TARF prices asked by different issuers tend to converge. This makes the promotion of TARF solely on price less effective to both investor and issuer. Therefore, in recent yearly, the focus is switched to post sales customer services.

8.4   Post sales customer services

Most investors of TARFs do not equip with an intelligent cash flow management system to keep track the realized and potential cash flows from their TARFs. These investors rely heavily on customer services from the issuer to advise the cash flows realized recently and potential cash flows to be realized in the near future. Thus investor friendly customer services are in high demand.

Nevertheless, professional customer services create a substantial operating overhead to an issuer since every TARF comprises many payoffs with variable cash flows. Therefore, computerized customer services are employed in order to differentiate their service qualities with other lower tier issuers. Through computer systems, an issuer is able to respond to an investor's enquiry within a short period of time in a professional manner. This help promotes the subsequent sales of other TARFs and/or investment products.

9   Valuation

The value of a TARF is the raw material cost for synthesizing a TARF in the foreign exchange market with the underlying currency, forwards and/or options. This value can never be observed from the market since the corresponding observable TARF price has always incorporated the value of the TARF, the operating cost and the profit to the issuer. In many situations, a TARF is synthesized to zero value. This makes the TARF price even less relevant to the generic value of a TARF.

The value of a TARF is calculated as the sum of all probability weighed discounted cash flows in domestic currency. The cash flows are specified by the payoff of each component option. The probabilities are largely controlled by the spot currency rate, strike rate, volatility and bonus target. The discount factors are determined by the maturities of component options and the interest rates of domestic currency.

9.1   Major valuation factors

The major factors which impact the value of a TARF are listed in Table 9.1.

	Bull TARF	Bear TARF
Call notional principal	+	-
Put notional principal	-	+
Strike rate	-	+
Bonus target	+	+
Aggregated bonus	-	-
Spot currency rate	+	-
Volatility	- (for the common construction where the put notional principal is substantially larger than the call notional principal)	- (for the common construction where the call notional principal is substantially larger than the put notional principal)

Table 9.1   Major factors impacting the value of a TARF

9.2   Monte Carlo simulation

This section describes the detailed procedures for valuating a TARF with Monte Carlo simulation. To simplify the presentation, a number of abbreviations are introduced in Table 9.2.

	Abbreviation	Description
1.	S_0	Spot currency rate on the valuation day
2.	σ	Daily volatility
3.	r_d	Daily domestic risk-free rate
4.	r_f	Daily foreign risk-free rate
5.	K	Strike rate
6.	t	Fixing day
7.	T_{Cal}	Number of calendar days between the valuation day and fixing day
8.	T_{Trad}	Number of trading days between the valuation day and fixing day
9.	T_{Pay}	Number of calendar days between the valuation day and two trading days after the fixing day
10.	N(0,1)	A random number drawn from the standard normal distribution

Table 9.2   Abbreviations

9.2.1   Market data

The spot currency rate, daily volatility, daily domestic risk-free rate and daily foreign risk-free rate are required market data to be input to the Monte Carlo simulation. The daily volatility is calculated by dividing a representative volatility (e.g. the ATM volatility with a tenor largely equal to the maturity of the TARF) on the volatility surface by the square root of the number of trading days in the following year. The daily domestic risk free rate is calculated by dividing a representative domestic risk-free rate (e.g. three-month or one-year interbank rate) along the term structure of domestic interest rate by the number of calendar days in the following year. The daily foreign risk-free rate is calculated by dividing a representative foreign risk-free rate (e.g. three-month or one-year interbank rate) along the term structure of foreign interest rate by the number of calendar days in the following year.

9.2.2   Fixing days and payment days

A fixing day is the day on which a pair of component call and put options mature and the payoffs of the two component options are calculated. The fixing days are calculated backward in accordance with the maturity day of the TARF and the fixing frequency.

The last fixing day is the same as the maturity day of the TARF. For a TARF with monthly fixing frequency, the second last fixing day is one month before the last fixing day and the third last fixing day is two months before the last fixing day. For a TARF with weekly fixing frequency, the second last fixing day is one week before the last fixing day and the third last fixing day is two weeks before the last fixing day. If any fixing day falls on a non-trading day, the fixing day is shifted to the following trading day.   The same scheme is applied to calculate other fixing days.

The payment day is the day on which the payoffs of the two component options are settled between the investor and issuer. For each fixing day, the payment is delivered on the second trading day after the fixing day.

9.2.3 Simulation

The following paragraphs set out the procedures for one simulation trial in the Monte Carlo simulation.

(a) Simulated currency rate

On every fixing day, a currency rate is simulated according to the following formula:

$$S_t = S_0 \exp\left[(r_d - r_f) T_{Cal} - \frac{\sigma^2 T_{Trad}}{2} + \sigma \sqrt{T_{Trad}} \times N(0,1) \right]$$

(b) Call payoff

On every fixing day, the payoff of a call option is calculated as

Payff[Call] = Max[S_t - K, 0] × Call notional principal

(c) Put payoff

On every fixing day, the payoff of a put option is calculated as

Payff[Put] = Max[K - S_t, 0] × Put notional principal

(d) Bonus

The positive payoff received by the investor is referred to as bonus. These bonuses are aggregated over the life of the TARF. If the aggregated amount of the bonus is equal to or above the bonus target, the TARF terminates automatically after the fixing day.

(e) Fixing value

The present value of a call option before termination is

PV[Call] = Payff[Call] × exp[$(-r_d T_{Pay})$]

The present value of a put option before termination is

$$PV[Put] = Payff[Put] \times \exp(-r_d T_{Pay})$$

Before termination, the fixing value is the net present value between a pair of call and put options. After termination, the fixing value is zero.

Adjustment should be made to a fixing at which the termination bonus occurs according to the termination condition (full or capped). The sum of present values of all fixings then becomes the value of a TARF for this particular simulation trial.

9.2.4 Theoretical value

The above procedures are carried out for many simulation trials. The average of all simulated TARF values then becomes the theoretical value of a TARF.

A higher accuracy is resulted when the number of simulation trials increases. There is no strict rule which specifies the sufficiency of number of simulation trails. In practice, the number of simulations is selected such that the entire Monte Carlo simulation for valuating one TARF can be completed in three to five minutes.

10   Risk analysis

This section describes the major risks facing the investor and issuer of a TARF.

10.1   Market risk

Market risk is the potential loss of a TARF arising from the movement of the currency rate during the investment period. It is measured by the present value-at-risk ("PVaR") which is the present value of the potential loss of a TARF under an extreme market condition relative to the theoretical value of a TARF.

The PVaR is a by-product of valuation with Monte Carlo simulation. During the Monte Carlo simulation, for each simulation trial, a simulated value of a TARF is generated. Through out the entire Monte Carlo simulation, a large number of simulated values are generated. The difference between the average of the simulated values and the simulated value at an extremely small percentile (e.g. 1%) becomes the PVaR of a TARF. If all simulated values are recorded in an Excel worksheet, the PVaR can be calculated easily as

PVaR = Average(Simulated TARF values)
         - Percentile(Simulated TARF values, 1%)

Theoretically, for an investment in similar TARFs, a loss above this PVaR will occur once every hundred times. The PVaR is usually much larger than the bonus target.

10.2   Credit risk

Both the investor and issuer are subject to credit risk since either party may fail to pay the counterparty on a payment day. In practice, an investor will only enter a TARF with a reputable financial institution under a regulator's supervision to minimize the credit risk. Conversely, an issuer may enter TARFs with many investors of various creditworthiness. Therefore, credit risk control from the issuer on the investors is imposed through margining under which the margin amount deposited by the investor must be sufficient to cover the margin consumption arising from his investments in TARFs at all time. Otherwise, the investor will be called for additional margin amount or the issuer will convert the TARFs of the investor into cash to stop loss.

10.2.1 Margin amount

Margin amount is the total discounted value of high liquidity financial instruments that an investor has deposited to the issuer. For each high liquidity financial instrument, a haircut rate is applied to its market value. The sum of the market values after haircut then becomes the margin amount of an investor. The haircut rate increases with increasing volatility, decreasing liquidity and increasing time interval between two consecutive calculations of the margin amount, and is assigned by the issuer on per instrument class basis.

In case an investor fails to pay the issuer on the payment day in accordance with the terms and conditions set out in a TARF contract, the issuer will conduct fire sale on those high liquidity financial instruments deposited by the investor in order to compensate the unpaid amount.

10.2.2 Margin consumption

The margin consumption is calculated on per investor's portfolio basis. It is an estimate of the maximum loss of the TARF portfolio if an issuer decides to unwind the TARF portfolio of an investor.

There is no industry standard method to calculate the margin consumption of a TARF portfolio. Fortunately, since a TARF can be replicated by a portfolio of vanilla currency options, the standardized portfolio analysis of risk ("SPAN") methodology being used by many derivatives exchanges to calculate the margin consumption for a portfolio of derivatives can be adopted,

Under the SPAN methodology, the entire TARF portfolio is first divided into many sub-portfolios in accordance with the underlying currency. Then the margin consumption for each sub-portfolio is calculated, following the step below.

(a) Origination value

For each TARF, the origination value is simply the value of the TARF when the investor acquires the TARF. The sum of the origination values of the TARFs in the sub-portfolio then becomes the origination value of the sub-portfolio.

(b) Scenario value

The maximum potential change of the rate of the underlying currency between two margin calculation days (A) and the maximum potential change of the volatility of the underlying currency between two margin calculation days (B) are estimated. Then for each combination of the currency rate and volatility in Table 10.1, a scenario value of the sub-portfolio is calculated. This results in a total of sixteen scenario values.

	Currency rate	Volatility
1.	Spot rate	Currency volatility + B
2.	Spot rate	Currency volatility - B
3.	Spot rate + A/3	Currency volatility + B
4.	Spot rate + A/3	Currency volatility - B
5.	Spot rate - A/3	Currency volatility + B
6.	Spot rate - A/3	Currency volatility - B
7.	Spot rate + 2A/3	Currency volatility + B
8.	Spot rate + 2A/3	Currency volatility - B
9.	Spot rate - 2A/3	Currency volatility + B
10.	Spot rate - 2A/3	Currency volatility - B
11.	Spot rate + A	Currency volatility + B
12.	Spot rate + A	Currency volatility - B
13.	Spot rate + A	Currency volatility + B
14.	Spot rate - A	Currency volatility - B
15.	Spot rate + 3A	Currency volatility
16.	Spot rate - 3A	Currency volatility

Table 10.1   Sixteen SPAN scenarios

(c) Scenario loss

For each scenario, the scenario loss is the difference between the origination value and the scenario value. The maximum of

- scenario losses for scenario 1 to 14; and

- 32% of scenario losses for scenarios 15 and 16,

then becomes of the margin consumption of the sub-portfolio.

The above calculation of margin consumption is repeated for each sub-portfolio. The sum of margin consumptions for all sub-portfolios then becomes the margin consumption for the entire TARF portfolio.

10.3   Operational risk

On a payment day, if the cash flow of a fixing cannot be settled or settled incorrectly, then a settlement failure occurs. This may result in a legal claim from the investor. The settlement failure is the primary operational risk due to the variation of cash flow amount in each fixing.

The operational risk is controlled by a fixing ticket which is prepared on the fixing day to the investor by the issuer. The fixing ticket lists

- the major identification details of a TARF;
- the settlement action and cash flow on the payment day;
- how the cash flow is calculated; and
- the aggregated bonus amount vs the bonus target.

10.4   Liquidity risk

Since a TARF is customized in accordance with the subjective view and preference of an investor, there is no secondary market in which an investor can dispose a TARF to another investor quickly. Therefore, a TARF is subject to a higher liquidity risk.

In order to unwind a TARF, an investor may enter a reverse transaction which matches the outstanding cash flows and bonus target of an original TARF in the opposite direction to offset the cash flows of the original TARF. Nevertheless, the investor must pay the operating cost and the profit to the issuer of the reversal TARF. This may result in a substantial cost to the investor.

10.5   Legal risk

When an investor acquires a TARF from an issuer, both parties are required to sign a deal confirmation which describes in legal terms the rights and obligations of both parties.

A typical deal confirmation comprises the specification of a TARF (set out in section 5), the schedule and calculation of cash flows and the risk disclosure to the investor.

There is no standardized template of deal confirmation for a TARF. Each issuer may have its own template of deal confirmation. As such, legal risk may arise in case the deal confirmation embeds any grey area which results in argument between the investor and issuer due to their different interpretations.

11   Derivative accounting

When an investor acquires a TARF from an issuer, the issuer should book the probability weighted values of each component options in its general ledger. For a TARF with N fixings, a total of N call options and N put options should be registered on the payment days. The probability weighted values of component options are also derived as a by-product with Monte Carlo simulation described in section 9.

During the Monte Carlo simulation, for each option, a large number of simulated present values are derived. The average of the simulated present values of an option then becomes the probability weighted value of the option.

12   Variations of TARF

A number of variations of TARF are designed to meet the risk-return preferences of various types of investors. This section describes four most popular variations.

12.1   Dual-strike TARF

Most TARF investors concern the situation where the currency rate moves against their expectation and results in leveraged loss on the fixing days. As a result, a dual-strike TARF is designed to address this concern of leveraged loss.

A dual-strike TARF is a TARF with its call options subject to a call strike rate and put options subject to a put strike rate where the call strike rate is always higher than the put strike rate.

12.1.1 Bull dual-strike TARF

For a bull dual-strike TARF, on the fixing day, if the currency rate is

- above the call strike rate, the investor receives from the issuer the payoff

    (Currency rate - Call strike rate) × Call notional principal

- below the put strike rate, the investor delivers to the issuer the payoff

(Put strike rate - Currency rate) × Put notional principal

- between the call and put strike rates, there is no payoff to either party.

A bull dual-strike TARF is designed for an investor who prefers a zero cost TARF and without leverage on the loss in case the currency rate drops below the put strike rate on the fixing day. While the put strike rate remains as the boundary which the investor expects that the currency rate will unlikely drops below during the investment horizon, the investor selects a higher call strike rate only starting from which a profit will be received and gives up the potential profit at the range between the call and put strike rates.

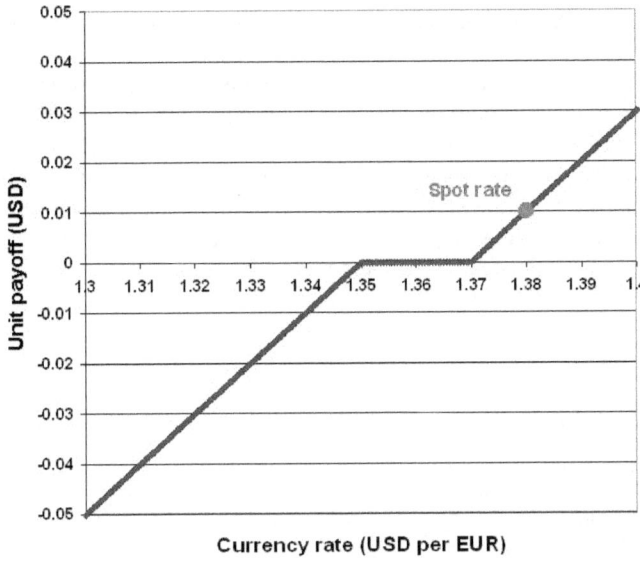

Figure 12.1   Unit payoff of a bull dual-strike TARF

This reduction in potential profit will reduce substantially the cost of the call options. The reduced call options cost is matched by a smaller revenue from selling put options with a smaller notional principal. Since the put notional principal is reduced, in case the currency rate is below the put strike rate on the fixing day, the loss is also reduced.

During the structuring of many bull dual-strike TARFs, the put strike rate is set according to the investor's view on the movement of the currency rate during the investment period, the call and put notional principals are equal, and the call strike rate and bonus target are selected to result in a near zero TARF value.

12.1.2 Bear dual-strike TARF

For a bear dual-strike TARF, on the fixing day, if the currency rate is

- below the put strike rate, the investor receives from the issuer the payoff

  (Put strike rate - Currency rate) × Put notional principal

- above the call strike rate; the investor delivers to the issuer the payoff

  (Currency rate - Call strike rate) × Call notional principal

- between the call and put strike rates, there is no payoff to either party.

A bear dual-strike TARF is designed for an investor who prefers a zero cost TARF and without leverage on the loss in case the currency rate rises above the call strike rate on the fixing day. While the call strike rate remains as the boundary which the investor expects that the currency rate will unlikely rises above during the investment horizon, the investor selects a lower put strike rate only starting from which a profit will be received and gives up the potential profit at the range between the call and put strike rates.

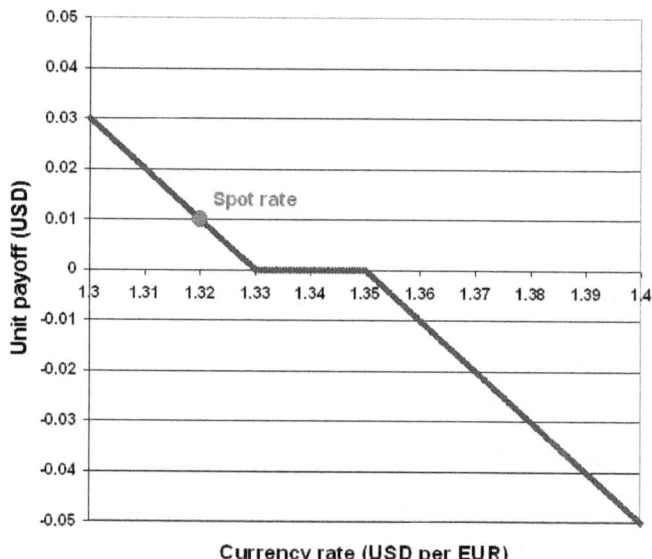

Figure 12.2   Unit payoff of a bear dual-strike TARF

This reduction in potential profit will reduce substantially the cost of the put options. The reduced put options cost is matched by a smaller revenue from selling call options with a smaller notional principal. Since the call notional principal is reduced, in case the currency rate is above the call strike rate on the fixing day, the loss is also reduced.

During the structuring of many bear dual-strike TARFs, the call strike rate is set according to the investor's view on the movement of the currency rate during the investment period, the call and put notional principals are equal, and the put strike rate and bonus target are selected to result in a near zero TARF value.

12.2   Survival gap TARF

A survival gap TARF is designed for an investor who has more concern on the loss when investing in a TARF. This investor seeks to minimize the probability of loss with a survival gap incorporated.

To minimize the probability of loss, a gap rate is created such that

- for a bull TARF, the loss will occur only if the currency rate moves below a gap rate lower than the strike rate; and

- for a bear TARF, the loss will occur only if the currency rate moves above a gap rate higher than the strike rate.

12.2.1 Bull survival gap TARF

For a bull survival gap TARF, on the fixing day, if the currency rate is

- above the strike rate, the investor receives from the issuer the payoff

    (Currency rate - Strike rate) × Call notional principal

- below the gap rate, the investor delivers to the issuer the payoff

    (Put strike rate - Strike rate) × Put notional principal

- between the strike and gap rates, there is no payoff to either party.

A survival gap is created below the strike rate such that even if the currency rate moves slightly below the strike rate, there will be no loss to the investor as long as the currency rate remains above the gap rate.   This essentially reduces the probability of loss. Nevertheless, since the payoff and cost of the call options remain unchanged, the reduction in probability of loss must be compensated by a larger put notional principal and/or smaller bonus target in order to maintain the TARF at zero value.

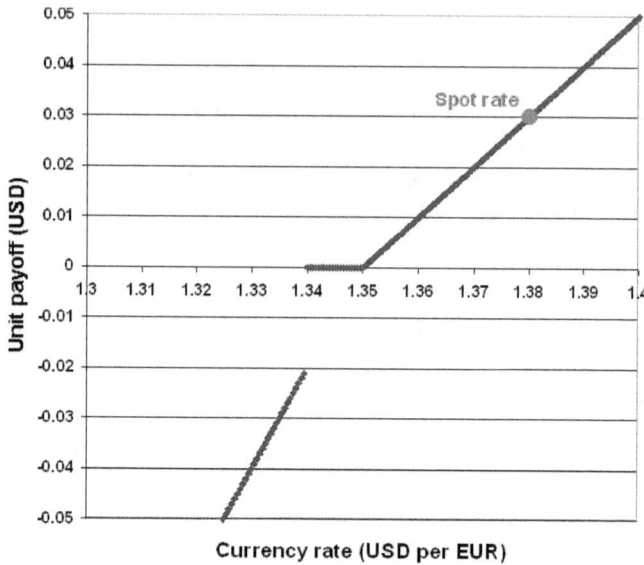

Figure 12.3   Unit payoff of a bull survival gap TARF

During the structuring of many bull survival gap TARFs, the strike rate is set according to the investor's view on the movement of the currency rate during the investment period, the put notional principal is equal to twice the call notional principal, and the gap rate and bonus target are selected to result in a near zero TARF value.

12.2.2 Bear survival gap TARF

For a bear survival gap TARF, on the fixing day, if the currency rate is

- below the strike rate, the investor receives from the issuer the payoff

  (Put strike rate - Strike rate) × Put notional principal

- above the gap rate; the investor delivers to the issuer the payoff

  (Currency rate – Strike rate) × Call notional principal

- between the strike and gap rates, there is no payoff to either party.

A survival gap is created above the strike rate such that even if the currency rate moves slightly above the strike rate, there will be no loss to the investor as long as the currency rate remains below the gap rate.   This essentially reduces the probability of loss.   Nevertheless, since the payoff and cost of the put options remain unchanged, the reduction in probability of loss must be compensated by a larger call notional principal and/or smaller bonus target in order to maintain the TARF at zero value.

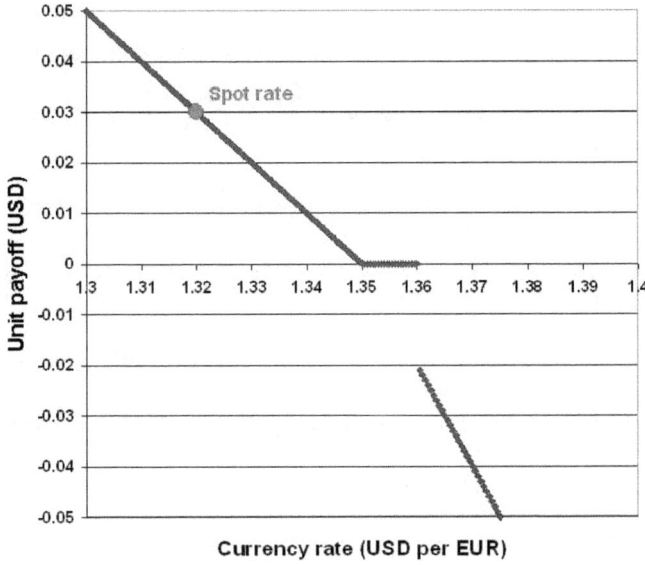

Figure 12.4   Unit payoff of a bear survival gap TARF

During the structuring of many bear survival gap TARFs, the strike rate is set according to the investor's view on the movement of the currency rate during the investment period, the call notional principal is equal to twice the put notional principal, and the gap rate and bonus target are selected to result in a near zero TARF value.

12.3   Pivot TARF

A pivot TARF is essentially a combination of

- a bull TARF with a lower strike rate. In addition, a pivot rate above the lower strike rate is selected such that if the currency rate is above the pivot rate, the bull TARF will deliver a zero payoff on the fixing day; and

- a bear TARF with an upper strike rate above the pivot rate. In addition, if the currency rate is below the pivot rate, the bear TARF will deliver a zero payoff on the fixing day.

A pivot TARF is designed for an investor to speculate on his view at a lower cost that a currency rate will move between a lower strike rate and an upper strike rate during the investment horizon.

For a pivot TARF, on the fixing day, if the currency rate is

- below the lower strike rate, the investor delivers to the issuer the payoff

  (Lower strike rate - Currency rate) × Lower put notional principal

- between the lower strike and pivot rates, the investor receives from the issuer the payoff

  (Currency rate - Lower strike rate) × Lower call notional principal

- between the pivot and upper strike rates, the investor receives from the issuer the payoff

  (Upper strike rate - Currency rate) × Upper put notional principal

- above the upper strike rate, the investor delivers to the issuer the payoff

  (Currency rate - Upper strike rate) × Upper call notional principal

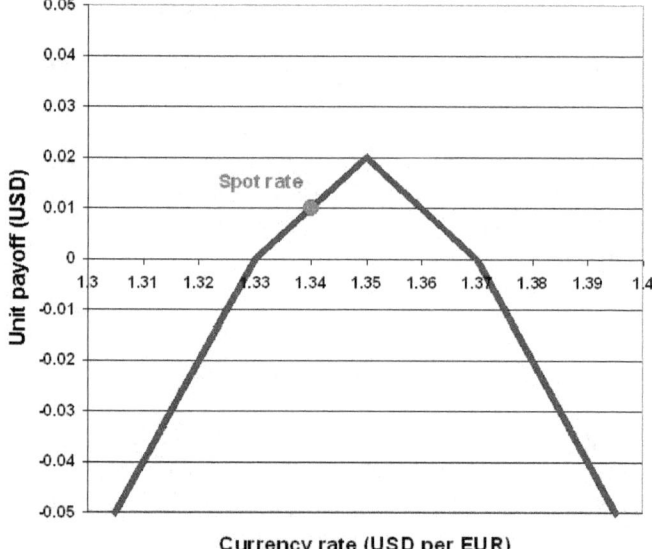

Figure 12.5   Unit payoff of a pivot TARF

During the structuring of many pivot TARFs, the lower and upper strike rates are set according to the investor's view on the movement of the currency rate during the investment period, the lower put notional principal is equal to twice the lower call notional principal, the upper call notional principal is equal to twice the upper put notional principal, and the pivot rate and bonus target are selected to result in a near zero TARF value.

A TARF originated with the pivot rate close to the spot currency rate allows an investor to speculate on the stability of the underlying currency. If the stability of the underlying currency is high, the currency rate will remain around the pivot rate throughout the investment horizon and a positive payoff will be resulted from either a lower call option or an upper put option on the fixing day.

12.4   Variable strike TARF

Recently due to the higher volatility in the currency market, some investors demand a TARF with different strike rates on different fixing days. These strike rates are selected to minimize the potential loss and maximize the potential profit on individual fixing basis, taking into account the expectation of the currency rate movements during different stages within a continuous investment horizon. This variable strike rate arrangement may apply to vanilla TARF, dual-strike TARF, survival gap TARF and pivot TARF.

Appendix 1   Sample fixing ticket

FIXING TICKET

Trade Identification	2373394638
Trade Date	08 August 2008
Structured Product	Target accrual redemption forward
Calculation Agent	Profit Bank
Fixing Date	07 November 2008
Fixing Time	4:00 pm
Pricing Source	Reuters page EURFIX01
Fixing Rate	1.36 USD per EUR

This fixing ticket is issued to notify Beta Technology Limited the fixing result of the trade 2373394638 on the fixing day 07 November 2008.

Fixing result

The Fixing Rate is 1.36 USD per EUR, which is above the Strike Rate 1.35 USD per EUR. Beta Technology Limited will buy from Profit Bank on payment day 09 November 2008 EUR 10,000,000 at the Strike Rate 1.35 USD per EUR.

After this fixing, the aggregated bonus is USD 612,000. The bonus target is USD 3,000,000

Appendix 2   Sample deal confirmation

DEAL CONFIRMATION

The purpose of this deal confirmation ("Confirmation") is to set out the terms and conditions of 12 currency transactions ("Transactions") entered into between Profit Bank Limited and Beta Technology Limited on the trade date specified below.

The definitions and provisions contained in the 1998 Foreign Exchange and Currency Option Definitions (as published by the International Swaps and Derivatives Association, Inc.; EMTA, Inc.; and Foreign Exchange Committee) are incorporated into this Confirmation. In the event of any inconsistency between those definitions and provisions and this Confirmation, this Confirmation will govern.

1. This Confirmation supplements, forms part of, and subject to, the ISDA Master Agreement dated as of 18 June 1993 as amended and supplemented from time to time ("Agreement"), between Profit Bank Limited ("Part A") and Beta Technology Limited ("Party B"). All provisions contained in the Agreement govern this Confirmation except as expressly modified below.

2. The terms of each Transaction to which this Confirmation relates are as follows:

Trade Identification	2373393784
Trade Reference	As stated in the Schedule attached hereto
Trade Date	08 August 2008
Currency and amount payable by Party A	In respect of a Transaction (subject to the Target Accrual Reduction Feature and Conditions)
	where Condition 1 is satisfied, the relevant amount in EUR ("EUR Amount 1") shown in the column "EUR Amount 1" in the Schedule attached hereto; or
	where Condition 2 is satisfied, the relevant amount in EUR ("EUR Amount 2") shown in the column "EUR Amount 2" in the Schedule attached hereto.

Currency and amount payable to Party B	In respect of a Transaction (subject to the Target Accrual Redemption Feature and Conditions), where Condition 1 is satisfied, the relevant amount in USD equal to the product of (i) the Strike Rate; and (ii) the relevant EUR Amount 1; or where Condition 2 is satisfied, the relevant amount in USD equal to the product of (i) the Strike Rate; and (ii) the relevant EUR Amount 2.
Settlement Date	In respect of a Transaction, two Hong Kong, New York and London Business Days following the relevant Determination Date, subject to the adjustment in accordance with the Following Business Day Convention.
Business days for Settlement Date	New York, London and Hong Kong
Calculation Agent	Party A

For the purposes of this Confirmation:

"Condition 1" means in respect of a Transaction, where EURmat fixes at or above the Strike Rate, subject to the Target Accrual Redemption Feature and Conditions.

"Condition 2" means in respect of a Transaction, where EURmat fixes below the Strike Rate, subject to the Target Accrual Redemption Feature and Conditions.

"EURmat" means in respect of a Transaction, the currency rate expressed as the amount of USD required to buy one EUR, as displayed on Reuters page EURFIX01 at or about 4:00 pm, London time on the relevant Determination Date. If such rate is not available for whatever reason, the rate as determined by the Calculation Agent in good faith and in a commercially reasonable manner is used.

"Strike Rate" means 1.35 USD per EUR.

"Determination Date" means in respect of a Transaction, the relevant Determination Date specified as such in Schedule attached hereto, subject to adjustment in accordance with Following Business Day Convention. In respect of a Determination Date, "Business Day" means, London and Hong Kong.

3. Target Accrual Redemption Feature and Conditions:

(a)   If Party B's Accumulative Positive Gain reaches USD 3,000,000 on any Determination Date, the relevant Transaction shall be terminated on the relevant Determination Date (such Determination Date, the "Termination Date").

(b)   Upon such termination and in respect of that Transaction, the relevant EUR Amount 1 shall be adjusted to a new amount ("Varied EUR Amount") in order to maintain the maximum Accumulative Positive Gain to the Target Accrual Redemption Level, as determined by the Calculation Agent. On the relevant Settlement Date, the amount payable to Party A in respect of the Transaction shall be the Varied EUR Amount and Party B shall pay an amount in USD equal to the product of (i) the Varied EUR Amount; and (ii) the Strike Rate;

(c)   Except for the amount described in (b) above and other amounts and payments due and payable prior and up to the Termination Date, all subsequent Transactions shall also be terminated and no further payment shall be required to be made by any party there under; and

(d)   Otherwise, there shall be no early termination of the Transactions if Party B's Accumulative Positive Gain is below the Target Accrual Redemption Level.

Monthly Gain	In respect of any Transaction, an amount in USD equal to the higher of
	(i) 10,000,000 multiplied by (EURamt on the relevant Determination Date - the Strike Rate); and
	(ii) zero.
Accumulative Positive Gain	In respect of any Transaction, the Monthly Gain of that Transaction plus the sum of all Monthly Gain respect of all Transaction(s) proceeding that Transaction.
Target Accrual Redemption Level	USD 3,000,000

4. Offices

The Office of Party A for these Transactions: Hong Kong

The Office of Party B for these Transactions: Hong Kong

5. Acknowledgement

Each party acknowledges that, in connection with these Transactions:

(i) Advice. It is not relying upon any advice (whether written or oral) of the other party to these Transactions, other than the representations expressly set forth in the Agreement.

(ii) Decisions. It has made its own decisions regarding the entering into these Transactions based upon this own judgment and upon advice from such of this own professional advisers as it has deemed necessary to consult.

(iii) Understanding. It understands the terms, conditions and risks of these Transactions and is willing to assume (financially and otherwise) those risks; and

(iv) Acting as principal. It is entering into these Transactions and such other documentation as principal, and not as agent or in any other capacity, fiduciary or otherwise.

SCHEDULE TRANSACTIONS

Transaction no.	EUR Amount 1	EUR Amount 2	Determination Date
1	EUR 10,000,000	EUR 20,000,000	10 September 2008
2	EUR 10,000,000	EUR 20,000,000	09 October 2008
3	EUR 10,000,000	EUR 20,000,000	07 November 2008
4	EUR 10,000,000	EUR 20,000,000	10 December 2008
5	EUR 10,000,000	EUR 20,000,000	08 January 2009
6	EUR 10,000,000	EUR 20,000,000	10 February 209
7	EUR 10,000,000	EUR 20,000,000	10 March 2009
8	EUR 10,000,000	EUR 20,000,000	08 April 2009
9	EUR 10,000,000	EUR 20,000,000	08 May 2009
10	EUR 10,000,000	EUR 20,000,000	10 June 2009
11	EUR 10,000,000	EUR 20,000,000	09 July 2009
12	EUR 10,000,000	EUR 20,000,000	10 August 2009

References

ALLRIGHT (2012). Target redemption forwards within Bloomberg: TARF description plus new variations of TARF.

CHAN & WONG (2013). Handbook of financial risk management: simulations and case studies.

LAM, KWAN & LAI (2014). Managing credit risk under the Basel III framework, 2nd edition.

Intercontinental Exchange (2014). SPAN margin system.

MANUEL & VEIGA (2004). Expanding further the universe of exotic options closed pricing formulas in the Black and Scholes framework.

STOIMENOV & WILKENS (2005). Are structured products 'fairly' priced? An analysis of the German market for equity-linked instruments.

CapitaLogic Limited

Empowering Wealth and Capital

CapitaLogic Limited ("CapLogic") provides financial technology advisory services and delivers corporate and private banking solutions to major banks in Asia. Since 1996, CapLogic has been developing and implementing cutting edged solutions to financial institutions in Hong Kong, Taipei, Shanghai, Macau, Singapore, Tokyo and Sydney, the monetary centres in the Asia Pacific region. Our staff comprise finance professionals with doctoral degree, CFA, CAIA, FRM, PRM and CPA qualifications.

Today, CapLogic is one of the only few pioneers in the region specializing in:

- structured products,
- CNY and CNH treasury businesses, and
- traditional and simplified Chinese interfaces.

Our flagships include: (i) WealthStructures, which facilitates the portfolio management and customer services of structured products; (ii) WealthEnquiry, which enables a bank's customer to oversee his portfolio of structured products over the Internet; and (iii) WealthAnalytics, which calculates the theoretical value, component cost, margin requirement and value-at-risk of structured products.

To contact CapitaLogic Limited

Address Room1501 Bangkok Bank Building,
        28 Des Voeux Road Central,
        Central, Hong Kong

Tel. no. (852) 2858 4190

E-mail cs@caplogic.com

Website www.caplogic.com

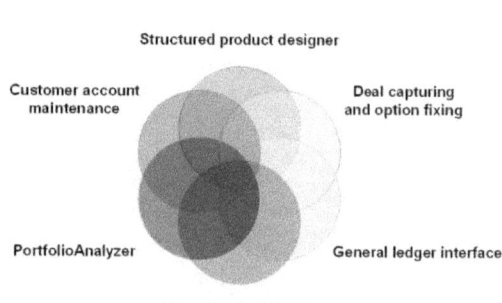

www.ingramcontent.com/pod-product-compliance
Lightning Source LLC
Chambersburg PA
CBHW071020180526
45168CB00003B/1496